Drawn from the Archive
Hidden Histories of Illustration

progressive roughs and final artwork
...raig for *Angelina Ballerina* (1983)

This book is dedicated to all the illustrators, authors and other donors who have so generously entrusted their archives to Seven Stories.

'Every book has a private history of its own, both of its conception and its execution – and some of those histories turn out to be passing strange.'

Brian Alderson, 'Words about Pictures: The Primacy of Text', *Books for Keeps*, No. 146, May 2004.

Author: Sarah Lawrance
Foreword: Dame Jacqueline Wilson
Art Director: Deirdre McDermott
Production Director: Alan Lee
Designer: Sarah Pannasch

The moral rights of the author have been asserted

First published in Great Britain in 2015 by Seven Stories Publications,
30 Lime Street, Ouseburn Valley, Newcastle upon Tyne NE1 2PQ
www.sevenstories.org.uk

A CIP catalogue record for this book is available from the British Library

ISBN 978-0-9928827-0-9

This book has been typeset in Bodoni Egyptian Pro and Frutiger

Printed and bound in Turkey by Ertem Ltd

10 9 8 7 6 5 4 3 2 1

Final artwork by Edward Ardizzone for *The Little Train* (1973)

Drawn from the Archive

Hidden Histories of Illustration

Sarah Lawrance

with a foreword by
Jacqueline Wilson

seven stories
National Centre for Children's Books

welcome!

Jacqueline Wilson

One of my favourite books as a child was *Ballet Shoes* by Noel Streatfeild. I pretended I was a fourth sister to the Fossil girls and pranced around our flat in my pink bedroom slippers. I read that little Puffin paperback so many times that its green cover disintegrated.

When I picked up a copy of *Ballet Shoes* as an adult I felt a wave of warm nostalgia. Not only did I know the text almost by heart, but also the black and white illustrations by Ruth Gervis were still wonderfully familiar because I had copied them many times and used them as inspiration for my imaginary games.

I also loved Shirley Hughes's illustrations for Noel Streatfeild's *The Bell Family*, probably one of her earliest commissions. I admired the way she drew Ginnie Bell's wispy plaits and bunchy gym tunic, making her look so touchingly real. It was wonderful to discover Shirley Hughes's warm colourful picture books many years later when my daughter was little. *Lucy and Tom's Day* was a particular favourite. Emma loved looking at the gentle everyday world of the two children.

Judith Kerr's *The Tiger Who Came to Tea* was another hugely popular choice when Emma was young. She did her best to paint her own magnificent stripy tiger when she was at nursery school.

I collect first editions of beautifully illustrated children's books now. I adore the subtle palette and sensitive solemn people created by Harold Jones. I love modern illustrators too, and have several of Angela Barrett's beautiful water-colours hanging at home.

I have an entire wall of Nick Sharratt's marvellous depictions of my child characters, from Tracy Beaker to Hetty Feather. Nick's artwork is universally loved by children. Almost every child's letter sent to me includes a Nick-style drawing. It's lovely to know that modern children care so much about illustration.

Seven Stories contains wonderful work from all these personal favourite illustrators of mine, plus many more. Sarah Lawrance, the Collection Director who looks after the valuable Seven Stories archive, has written 25 extremely informative pieces about the illustrators, brimful of fascinating details.

This is a beautiful book to treasure, not just for children's literature experts, but for anyone who has ever responded joyfully to a particular picture in a book.

Right: *'Working at a model made in Meccano'*. Petrova Fossil from *Ballet Shoes* (1936), illustrated by Ruth Gervis

contents

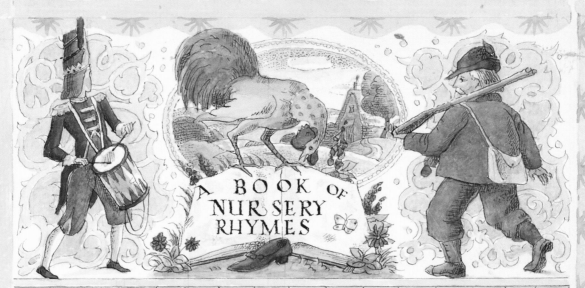

A BOOK OF
NURSERY
RHYMES

LAVENDER'S
BLUE

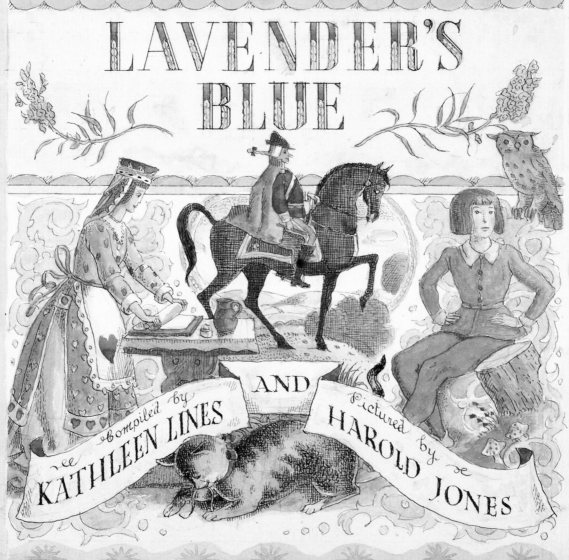

Compiled by
KATHLEEN LINES
AND
Pictured by
HAROLD JONES

1930s–1950s

'At his best, the good illustrator does more than just make a pictorial comment on the written word. He produces a visual counterpart which adds a third dimension to the book, making more vivid and more understandable the author's intention.'

Edward Ardizzone, 'The Born Illustrator', a talk for the
Double Crown Club, 1958. Quoted by Judy Taylor Hough in
'Working with Ardizzone', an undated typescript in
the Kaye Webb archive at Seven Stories.

Facing page and above: final artwork by Harold Jones for the front cover of *Lavender's Blue* (1954)

Ballet Shoes

by Noel Streatfeild *(J.M. Dent & Sons, 1936)*

RUTH GERVIS *1894–1988*

Self-portrait of Ruth Gervis reproduced by courtesy of Paul Gervis and Nicolette Winterbottom

Bmallet Shoes is one of a handful of children's books from the 1930s to remain in print today with its original illustrations. Ruth Gervis's simple line drawings are a perfect match for the economy and pace of Noel Streatfeild's narrative, creating a memorable impression of the three Fossil sisters that has shaped the imaginations of generations of readers.

Ruth Gervis and Noel Streatfeild were sisters. Despite – or more likely because of – their austere vicarage upbringing, the girls loved their occasional visits to the theatre. When the children's dance troupe, Lila Fields's 'Little Wonders', came to town, the sisters were enchanted.

Facing page: *'They had a lovely time at Pevensey'.*
Finished artwork marked up for printing

15' 83%

166 mm

GERVIS.

14

They had a lovely time at Pevensey.

RG/01/01/31   Ballet Shoes

GERVIS.

Theo looked round for
the cause this joke

'Theo looked round for the cause of the joke'. Finished artwork marked up for printing

Like many women of their generation, Gervis and Streatfeild enjoyed the opportunity to pursue careers in a way that had been unthinkable before. Gervis became an artist, earning a comfortable living during the 1920s through painting and teaching. She began to take on extra work as an illustrator so that she could pay for a nanny, since – according to her daughter – she did not expect to be any good at looking after children.

The commission for *Ballet Shoes* came by chance; the editor at Dent had not even realised that Gervis and Streatfeild were related.

Despite the success of *Ballet Shoes*, Streatfeild's other books were almost all illustrated by other artists. Perhaps Gervis was too busy with other commissions – including titles by Enid Blyton and Kitty Barne, who, coincidentally, was a Streatfeild by marriage. In any case, as publishers increasingly requested pen and ink rather than pencil drawings, Gervis ceased to enjoy illustrating, and focused instead on teaching, which she loved.

In 1949, *Ballet Shoes* was re-published as a Puffin storybook and, priced one shilling and sixpence, was now affordable to many more children. Sadly, the quality of the reproduction did no favours to the subtlety of Gervis's pencil line. A comparison between the original drawings and the paperback reproduction shows just how much has been lost in translation.

Top left: Puffin paperback editions.
The original 1949 green cover (left)
and the 1957 reprint with pink cover (right)

Top right: *'We three Fossils [...] vow to try and put our name in history books because it's our very own and nobody can say it's because of our grandfathers.'*
The original pencil drawing (left) and the same drawing as reproduced in the paperback edition (right)

The Visit to the Farm *(Faber, 1939)*
The Enchanted Night *(Faber, 1947)*

HAROLD JONES *1904–1992*

Photograph of Harold Jones held in the OUP Archive, reproduced by permission of Oxford University Press

Harold Jones had toyed with becoming a farmer and spent a year working in Warwickshire, before realising his mistake and enrolling at art school instead. By the 1930s he was firmly established as a black and white illustrator, as well as teaching art students at Oxford and Chelsea.

In 1937 he won critical acclaim for *This Year, Next Year* – an anthology of poems, written by Walter de la Mare to accompany Jones's illustrations, for which he employed the new technique of colour autolithography.

Facing page: line drawings for *The Visit to the Farm*, marked up for printing

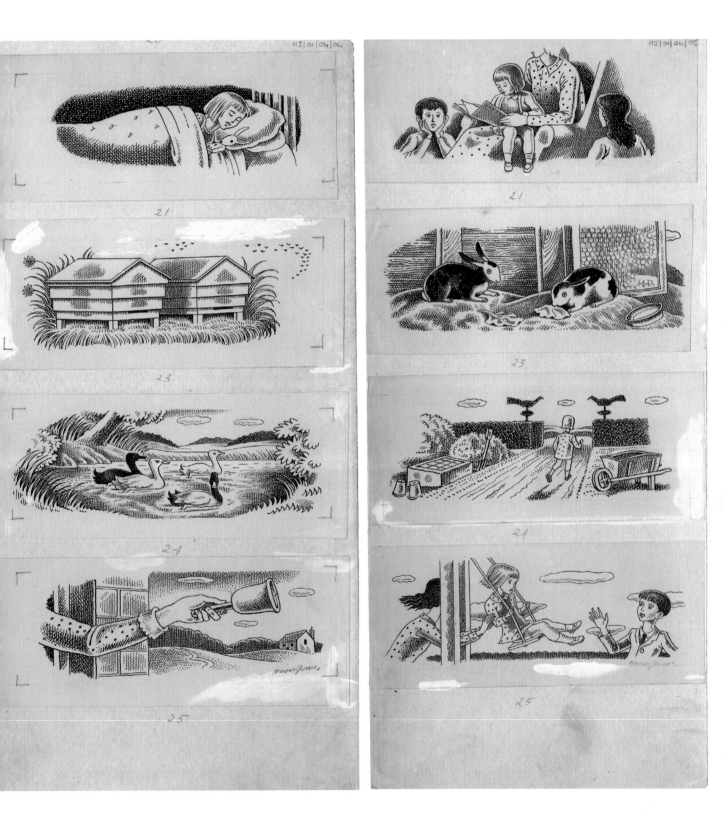

21

23

24

25

21

23

24

25

> *'an illustration should positively, even minutely – describe the text in every possible way: but it must go further than a prosaic description of the facts. I think illustration is dominated by a sense of rhythm, design, of parts relating to the whole – it's pattern making that intrigues me.'*

Harold Jones, quoted in the *Guardian*, December 1974.

'"Good-bye, Stephanie!" cried the children.'
Proof for one of the two-colour illustrations for *The Visit to the Farm*

By now Jones had two young daughters, to whom he had promised stories. *The Visit to the Farm*, featuring Stephanie Angela, appeared in 1939; the illustrations, in black and two colours, were reproduced by the less expensive line block technique. Both story and pictures are imbued with a nostalgic affection for country life and close observations of nature.

A reviewer writing in the *Church Times* hailed *The Visit to the Farm* as 'another nursery winner', describing pictures in the book as 'among some of the best drawn for children in recent years'. Billy Nichols (aged 4½) was more equivocal: 'I like it very much … but it would be better if she were called Janet instead of Stephanie Angela' (*Time and Tide*, December 1941). Jones kept all his reviews, carefully labelled and pasted into a notebook.

During the war Jones drew maps for the Supreme Headquarters of the Allied Expeditionary Force; he saw plans for the

Book cover designs by Harold Jones.
The Enchanted Night (this page) and
The Visit to the Farm (facing page)

D-Day invasion before the Generals.
There was no time for book illustration,
but the manuscript of the story for his
second daughter, *The Enchanted Night*,
is dated 1943. The book was finally
published in 1947.

Harold Jones's masterpiece is
Lavender's Blue (1954), an anthology of
nursery rhymes compiled by Kathleen
Lines, which he designed and illustrated
from end to end. While copies of *This
Year, Next Year* are now scarce because
the lithographic plates were re-used
during the war, such that no more copies
could be printed, happily *Lavender's Blue*
remains in print to this day.

Artwork by Harold Jones can be found
in several major collections, but, thanks
chiefly to the generosity of his daughters
Stephanie and Gabrielle, by far the largest
amount – for more than twenty books – is
now at Seven Stories.

THE ENCHANTED NIGHT

One - two - and THREE - solemnly,
from the shadowy corner of the room,
the old grandfather's clock chimed the
hour. Little Gabrielle Pamela stirred
in her sleep, and then slowly opened
her eyes. The room was bathed in
moonlight, and everything could be
seen almost as clearly as if it
were day. There propped up against
the wall, were Gabrielle's favourite
dolls, and beside them her much
loved puppy – and on the other side
stood her own little dressing table, with
her dressing gown lying across the chair.
The yellow moon beams added an air
of enchantment and mystery to everything
around. Gabrielle Pamela sat up in

Harold Jones's handwritten manuscript for *The Enchanted Night*,
dated July 1943

The Toys Come to Life

by Enid Blyton *(Brockhampton Press, 1943)*

EILEEN SOPER *1905–1990*

Noddy Goes to Toyland

by Enid Blyton *(Sampson Low, Marston & Co. Ltd, 1949)*

HARMSEN VAN DER BEEK *1897–1953*

Courtesy of Chris Beetles Gallery

Enid Blyton wrote over 700 books, most of which were illustrated. She was so commercially successful that publishers were – unusually – prepared to allow her to influence the choice of illustrators. Among her favourites were Eileen Soper and Harmsen Van der Beek.

Soper is best known as the original illustrator of the *Famous Five* series, which began in 1942. Like Blyton, Soper had a keen interest in the natural world – reflected in her extremely skilled and engaging depictions of plants and animals.

Courtesy of the Enid Blyton Society

Facing page: *'I would be greatly pleased if my collaboration could contribute to the success of your books.'* Letter from Van der Beek to Blyton, seeking approval for his interpretation of her Toytown characters

7 May 49

TOY TOWN

Dear Mrs. Blyton.

Herewith I have the honour to present to you in pictures little Noddy - Big Ears - Mr and Mrs Tubby and some other characters from your stories, which reached me through Mrs Sampson Low some days ago. I have thouroughly enjoyed reading them and I think they are extraordinary amusing, especially for an illustrator, because every line gives new inspiration for an illustration — I sent to Mrs. Sampson Low a series of sketches of the characters as above and I sinceraly hope that you'll like them, when you possibly have any particular ideas in your mind please let me know, as I can always make some alterations — I would be greatly pleased if my collaboration could contribute to the succes of your books.

Yours sincerely.

WITH COMPLIMENTS
HARMSEN VAN BEEK

'I have finished the first two Little Noddy books, and here they are. I have written them with a view to giving Van Beek all the scope possible for his particular genius – toys, pixies, market-places – he'll really enjoy himself…'

Enid Blyton writing to David White at Sampson Low, Marston & Company, March 1949. Quoted in Barbara Stoney, *Enid Blyton: The Biography*, London: Hodder & Stoughton, 1974, p. 158.

Despite her prolific output, remarkably little of Soper's Blyton artwork remains. It seems that publishers of this period often did not either preserve the original artwork or return it to the illustrator. Seven Stories' complete set of Soper's artwork for *The Toys Come to Life*, in watercolour on board, is certainly a very unusual survival.

The extraordinary success of Enid Blyton's 'Noddy' is surely due in large measure to the quality of the original illustrations by Dutch artist Harmsen Van der Beek. Beek had been introduced to Enid Blyton by the publisher Sampson Low in early 1949, because his style seemed ideally suited to the toy stories that they had in mind. Blyton was immediately inspired to write *Noddy Goes to Toyland* (1949) for Beek to illustrate.

His first detailed drawings of the Toyland characters appeared in a letter to the author dated 4 May 1949, which Blyton later kept framed above her desk. Over the next twenty years more than 154 Noddy books appeared. Though Beek died in 1953, he had done such a good job of establishing the characters that other artists were able to continue the series.

Gollies were popular toys in many homes during the 1940s, so it is not surprising that they feature prominently in both *The Toys*

Come to Life and the early Noddy stories. The original artwork is a startling reminder that this kind of racial caricature was once acceptable. In new editions of the Noddy stories, published during the 1990s, the gollies have been carefully edited out of both text and illustrations.

All the toy farm animals bent their heads and drank.

page 29

Facing page: artwork by Eileen Soper
for *The Toys Come to Life*

The kitchen cat pounces on a clockwork mouse
(above) and *'"Hurry, hurry!" said Golly.
"Don't take all night walking out!"'* (below)

This page: illustration by Van der Beek from
Here Comes Noddy Again (1951), the fourth title
in the Noddy series

The Little Train

by Graham Greene *(Eyre and Spottiswoode, 1946)*

DOROTHY CRAIGIE *1908–1971*

Courtesy of Oliver Walston

In dull and dreary post-war Britain, trains represented an escape from the everyday, a route to adventure and exploration – no wonder they also made popular children's book characters. Like Diana Ross's *Little Red Engine* (1942) and the Reverend W. Awdry's *Thomas the Tank Engine* (1946), Graham Greene's *Little Train* has a taste for big adventures. Early one morning, he runs away from the comfort and security of Little Snoreing, steaming down the main line, far from home, through the Great Gloomy Mountains, via Tombe Junction, to the dirty crowded environs of Smokeoverall. Here the engine's courage – and coal – fails him.

Facing page: contrasting cover designs by Craigie, 1946 (above) and Ardizzone, 1973 (below)

The Little Train

DOROTHY CRAIGIE

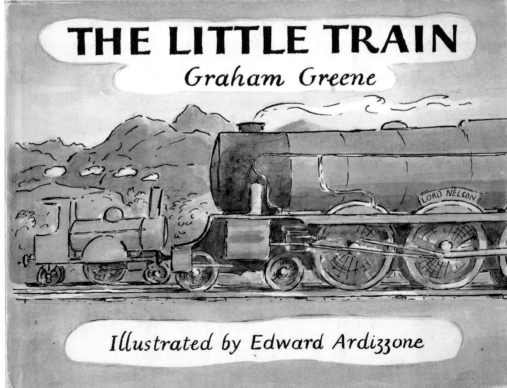

THE LITTLE TRAIN

Graham Greene

LORD NELSON

Illustrated by Edward Ardizzone

'"Goodbye branch line, I'm going where the great expresses are".' Final artwork

In the nick of time, he is rescued by 'the great Jock of Edinburgh, the famous Scottish express', who pushes him home to Little Snoreing, to a hero's welcome.

The Little Train was the first of four stories written by Greene for his sometime lover Dorothy Craigie to illustrate. As a director of Eyre & Spottiswoode, Greene was able to ensure publication – though his conflict of interests was discreetly concealed by attributing both text and illustrations to Craigie on the cover and title page of the first edition.

Craigie had previously worked as a theatre costume designer. Her artwork for *The Little Train* is in a strikingly modernist style: flat planes of colour, bold compositions and adventurous typographic layout. In 1957, Craigie re-styled the illustrations for a new edition of the book by Max Parrish, but by the late 1960s *The Little Train* was out of print.

'With a high squeal of fear from his funnel the little train bolted backwards.' Final artwork

Though Craigie and Greene had long since parted, Greene would not allow the story to be illustrated by anyone else. Finally, after Craigie died in 1971, Greene gave permission for *The Little Train* and the other three books in the series to be re-illustrated by his friend Edward Ardizzone, with characteristic warmth and an affectionate nostalgia for the age of steam.

Craigie's illustrations eventually found a new home with a private collector who admired her work, and subsequently donated them to Seven Stories. In 2010 Craigie's artwork was joined at Seven Stories by Ardizzone's, so that the two versions can now be seen side by side.

'Craigie's modernist-inflected images enhance the elements of risk and excitement.'

Kimberley Reynolds, 'Recoupling Text and Image: Graham Greene's The Little Train', *The Lion and the Unicorn*, vol. 37, No. 1, January 2013.

25

Tim and Charlotte *(Oxford University Press, 1951)*
Tim in Danger *(Oxford University Press, 1953)*

EDWARD ARDIZZONE *1900–1979*

Tim and Charlotte and *Tim in Danger* are fourth and fifth in the ten-book series which began in 1936 with *Little Tim and the Brave Sea Captain* and ended with *Ship's Cook Ginger* in 1977.

Each Little Tim story has certain common features: the period seaside setting; the characters; the dangers – usually shipwreck – narrowly averted. It might seem that Ardizzone was complacently repeating a successful formula. In fact, he was constantly revisiting and re-working, even between editions of the same story, to the extent that several of the early books were completely re-drawn to a different format.

Facing page: final artwork for the opening page of *Tim in Danger*, with text pasted on to kodatrace overlay

It was a lovely day when Tim, Charlotte and Ginger were playing on the beach. The sky was blue, the sea was blue, and the white yachts were sailing in the bay.

 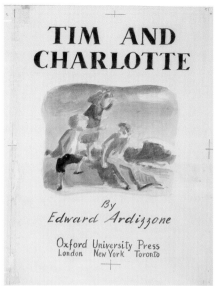 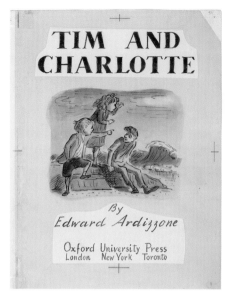

Final artwork for the title page of *Tim and Charlotte*, separated into its constituent
layers – ink on kodatrace (left); pencil and watercolour (centre); and both layers together,
forming the final image (right)

Ardizzone was continually searching
for the most faithful means of reproducing
his colour artwork. From 1949 (*Tim to the
Rescue*) until the early 1960s he favoured
the use of a 'kodatrace' overlay for his
black lines, with the pencil sketch and
watercolour on paper underneath. By lining
up the layers, using registration marks, the
final image appears.

The preparatory work for *Tim and
Charlotte* reveals that Ardizzone also
faced challenges with the text. In his first
dummy book, Charlotte (who has lost her
memory during a shipwreck) is reclaimed
by 'a horrid looking fat man' who professes

(falsely) to be her father. Tim and Ginger
uncover the sinister truth but, in order to
catch the fat man and his thin accomplice
red-handed, Charlotte has to allow herself
to be kidnapped. Whether Ardizzone
himself had second thoughts, or whether
somebody else intervened, is not known,
but in the final version the criminals are
replaced by well-meaning but dull Aunt
Agatha, who turns out to be the orphan
Charlotte's real guardian. This makes for
a less exciting but more palatable story; it
also means that the wonderful image of
Tim and Ginger spying on the fat man in
the pub is sadly lost.

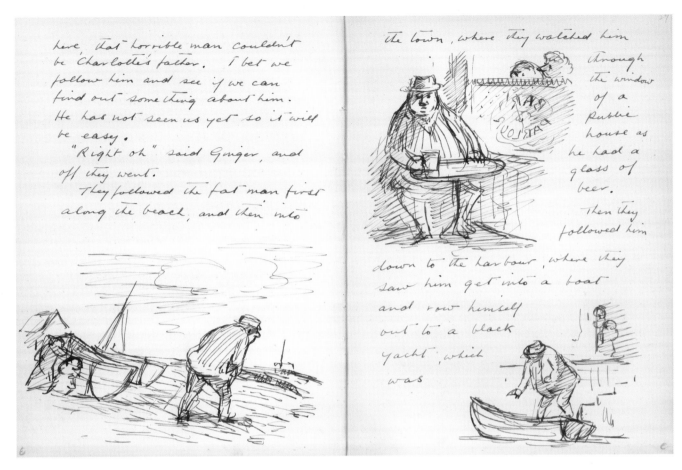

here, that horrible man couldn't be Charlotte's father. I bet we follow him and see if we can find out something about him. He has not seen us yet so it will be easy.

"Right oh" said Ginger, and off they went.

They followed the fat man first along the beach, and then into the town, where they watched him through the window of a public house as he had a glass of beer.

Then they followed him down to the harbour, where they saw him get into a boat and row himself out to a black yacht, which was

Early version of *Tim and Charlotte* showing Tim and Ginger spying on the fat man

'[Ardizzone's] child heroes and heroines are never allowed
any short-cuts, but must win through real difficulties
to achieve their happily-ever-afters.'

Grace Hogarth, 'Edward Ardizzone recalled
by his publisher', *The Sunday Times*, December 1979.

1960s–1980s

'The production of young children's books is of a very high standard. A quiet revolution has taken place … a few thin pages can nowadays cost 21s. and the old formula of maximum bulk, colour and 'value' has been replaced by some most sophisticated packages.'

Robert Denniston, 'A revolution in picture books', *Observer*, December 1966.

Final artwork by Jan Ormerod for *Sunshine* (1981, facing page) and front cover design (top)

Lucy and Tom's Day

(Victor Gollancz, 1960)

SHIRLEY HUGHES *Born 1927*

Most illustrators create a 'dummy' at an early stage when working on a new book. This can be just a few sheets of folded paper with roughly drawn illustrations, or more finished, depending on how it is going to be used. The dummy shows how many spreads will be needed (normally twelve spreads for a 32 page book) and how the page layouts will work, as well as the style and content of the illustrations. It is a working tool for the illustrator but it can also be shown to an editor, helping her to decide whether or not to publish the book, and to have a role in shaping it.

Facing page: front cover design from the dummy (above) and first edition by Victor Gollancz (below)

LUCY AND TOM'S DAY

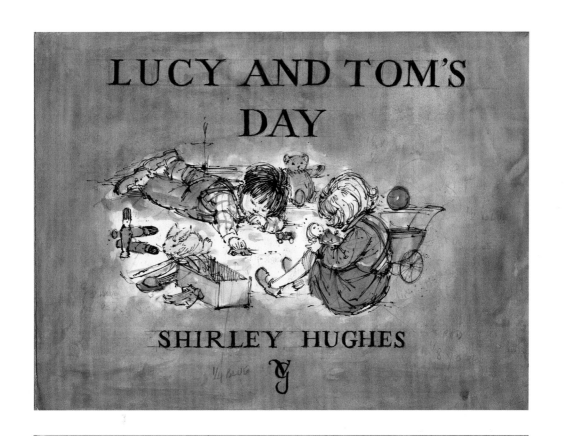

SHIRLEY HUGHES

LUCY AND TOM'S DAY

SHIRLEY HUGHES

After breakfast Lucy is very busy helping her mother about the house.
Tom especially enjoys making the beds.

Shirley Hughes was well-established as a black and white illustrator of other people's texts, but *Lucy and Tom's Day* was her first picture book, so it was important to demonstrate to the publisher that she knew what she was about. She had long nurtured the idea of a simple story about a typical day in the life of two small children, so the concept was well-developed: the layout and composition of the dummy are almost identical to the finished artwork.

In 1960, full-colour printing was still very expensive, so the normal pattern was for one side of the printed sheet to be in three or four colours, and the other side monochrome, to reduce costs. Hughes used the dummy to demonstrate how she would exploit this variation, and in particular how she would maximise the opportunities presented by the colour pages.

Hughes's drawings of children, in particular, have a freshness and energy

Top: *'Lucy is very busy helping her mother'*. Three-colour image from the dummy. Close, but not identical to, the final version, which is also in three colours

Three people usually call at Lucy and Tom's house before breakfast

the paper boy   the milkman   and the postman

that makes them look as though they were drawn directly from life. In fact this is not the case. Hughes is an habitual sketcher, in pencil and pen and ink, forever capturing movement, gesture and expression. This process of constant observation and drawing has laid down a memory bank of images that she can call upon at will; if she needs a specific visual reference for a figure, she looks to her sketchbooks for inspiration.

tricycles or doll's prams to the park, while they are playing the mothers like to sit on
the benches and talk a lot.

Top: *'the paper boy, the milkman and the postman'.* Black line on tracing paper. The brown marks are glue stains – a frequent occurrence in artwork from this period

Above: *'In the afternoon Lucy and Tom go to the park with their mother.'* Pencil sketch; the final image is in full colour

Mrs Cockle's Cat

by Philippa Pearce *(Constable, 1961)*

ANTONY MAITLAND *Born 1932*

While Philippa Pearce was already an established name – after winning the Carnegie medal for *Tom's Midnight Garden* (1958) – this was Antony Maitland's debut. A reviewer in *Junior Bookshelf* praised Maitland's work for its 'firm, positive style … vitality and a rich sense of humour' and hailed the book for being 'thoroughly contemporary and original' while belonging clearly to the English picture book tradition. *Mrs Cockle's Cat* went on to win the Kate Greenaway Medal for the best illustrated book published in 1961.

Facing page: trial version of cover artwork.
The final cover shows just the cat, not Mrs Cockle

Mrs. Cockle's Cat

Philippa Pearce

with drawings by Antony Maitland

CONSTABLE

Ironically, the English picture book scene was just about to change forever. From the mid-1960s, full-colour illustration, shorter texts and a 32-page format became the norm. *Mrs Cockle's Cat*, with its longer text and illustrations in black and white and two colours, seemed outdated and soon slipped out of print. In 1987, the book was re-issued in a series for young readers. The new version was smaller, paperback, ran to 62 pages (but with fewer lines to a page than the original), and had a completely new set of line drawings by Maitland.

Comparison between the two sets of illustrations – both held by Seven Stories – highlights the differences. In 1961, Maitland employed a mixture of ink and crayon, with interesting variations in depth and texture and in the thickness of the line; in the later drawings the penwork is smooth and even, with careful cross-hatching and firm outlines all combining to create cleaner but rather more static images. There is also a discernible impact on characterisation: the 1987 Mrs Cockle seems decidedly rounder, cheerier and less introspective than her predecessor. The change in style and technique was more than likely dictated by the new format – clarity of line being essential for good quality paperback reproduction and legibility by the young reader – but it is hard not to regret the loss of the sparky originality of the earlier, Medal-winning version.

Top: *'From the roof she could look round over the buildings of London.'* Trial version of colour artwork. In the final composition, Maitland drew Mrs Cockle emerging from the trapdoor with her basket of laundry, looking fondly at Peter instead of out at the view

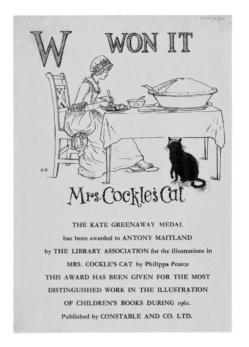

'Here is that rarest of books nowadays, a genuine English picture book, as English as Rowlandson or fish and chips.'

Junior Bookshelf, November 1961.

Top left: *'Old Mrs Cockle lived at the very top of a very tall house in London.'* Artwork from the first edition
Above: the same image, re-drawn for the 1987 edition

Charlie and the Chocolate Factory

by Roald Dahl *(George Allen and Unwin, 1967)*

FAITH JAQUES *1923–1997*

The Faith Jaques archive is full of stories. Notes and drawings from 1940s art school days through to the 1990s tell of a life's work in illustration. Files of reference material reveal her meticulously detailed picture research, while correspondence to and from a host of fellow illustrators, authors and other professional contacts reflects her tireless campaigning for better royalties for illustrators and a share in Public Lending Right.

Like many illustrators in the post-war period, Jaques made a living mainly from black and white drawings for newspapers and magazines, moving into book illustration in the mid-1960s.

Facing page: Puffin edition (1973), with cover artwork by Faith Jaques

Charlie and the Chocolate Factory

Roald Dahl

This was a boom-time for children's publishing and her style was well-suited to the demand for line-drawn chapter headings. She was particularly proud to have been the illustrator of the first British edition of Roald Dahl's *Charlie and the Chocolate Factory* (1967) and was devastated, some years later, to discover that the publisher – or possibly the printer – had lost all 45 of her drawings for the book; when the story was re-issued as a Puffin paperback, they had to make plates from photographs of the first edition, not from the artwork. Not only was it now impossible for any new edition to do justice to the quality of the illustrations, but also Jaques was unable to exhibit or sell the artwork – a valuable source of additional income for many illustrators. The experience fuelled her campaigning; as late as 1986 she wrote an impassioned letter to the magazine of the Society of Authors, entitled 'Gone Missing', in which she described the loss of the Charlie artwork as her 'first (and worst) disaster'.

The only original Jaques illustrations for *Charlie and the Chocolate Factory* that escaped are two drawings of Augustus Gloop which were not used in the book, enabling an interesting comparison between these and the final published version.

Left: three different versions of Faith Jaques's illustration of Augustus Gloop, finder of the first Golden Ticket. Unused variants (top and centre) and published version, for which the final artwork has been lost (bottom)

Facing page: manuscript draft of a letter (c.1967) from Faith Jaques to Roald Dahl, asking his advice about changing some of her illustrations for the Puffin edition to match the text

Dear Mr. Dahl — I had Puffin Books on the 'phone yesterday about the cover design for Charlie & the Choc. Factory. I rang you & was told you'll be back on Monday night, so thought it worth writing to you about it, as I don't want to agree to anything without ~~first~~ direction from you & A & U. ~~The~~ Do you want the same subject-matter on the Puffin cover as on the hardback? I had taken it for granted that I'd do the same scene, possibly re-grouped a bit because of differing dimensions — I felt that its very familiar to children, & seems right to me. Puffins will abide by whatever you say — so would you let me know if you want a version of the same scene or have some new ideas about it? Then I'll tell them & go ahead accordingly.

While I'm writing I'd better tell you of a problem the Puffin's reader has raised — my ears bill about the 2 replacement drawings of the Oompa-Loompas for the first "Charlie". Apparently be giving you about it on Tuesday morning. but its so complicated I think I might as well explain it to you the readers discovered my new drawings don't accord with the text, & to my horror I find she's right. ~~Its all rather complicated~~, & I'm at a slight disadvantage because presumably you must have written a new passage to ~~cover~~ the total change them from black to white & I don't know what it says. But apart from that P. 62 of Charlie I says (at foot of page) that the men wear deerskins, the women wear leaves & the children nothing at all. My ~~drawing~~ an original drawing on P. 60 just gets away with it, in that the clothes might be interpreted as skins — just! And on that page the group is clearly referred to as all men, so the women & children problem doesn't arise. And on P. 85 they're too tiny for it to matter.

So I'll need to know if the new version still refers to this group of 5 little men. ~~The reason why I not wrong~~ The thing is I put all the new O.L's, both for Charlie I & Charlie II in rather vague loin-cloth affairs, sometimes with a bit draped over one shoulder. Certainly not deerskins — as I realise now I should have done. So I'll have to alter this in the 2 replacement drawings (which, unless you've altered it, will still be all men.); & also those for Charlie II, the major one being the ½-page spread where hundreds of O.L's greet the return of the Elevator. ~~So~~ I'll alter the clothes to deerskins but the other issue is: do you want some changed to women & children? Among the notes I made while talking to you on the 'phone about Charlie & the GGE, I have this: "New Oompa-Loompas; jolly, gay, giggly, still small. all men. long-ish hair down to shoulders. ~~Pink faces, tiny~~"

The thing is I regard Allen & Unwin as my clients, & you as the person whose directions I should follow. I rang A & U ~~after all this~~ about it & they felt 'Puffins should have referred it all to Item first & they would have contacted you. (In fact Puffins sent a letter about it c/o the 2 originals ~~at~~ an address I haven't been at for 10 years! Jolly lucky they eventually got them all back — they're flapping now because they're about to go to press.) I'm quite happy to alter anything to accord with the text, I just need to be able to tell Puffins everything you've directed me to do. So the issues really are as follows:

(as in text P. 60)

1) Charlie & the Choc. Factory, pp. 60 & 85. Should these remain as men, but with ~~deerskins~~ not cloth garments? I made their hair shaggy & not clearing shoulders — Puffins seemed to feel it should be longer — does the newly-written passage imply much longer hair?

The Tiger Who Came to Tea

(William Collins Sons & Co. Ltd, 1968)

JUDITH KERR *Born 1923*

© Seven Stories National Centre for Children's Books

The Judith Kerr archive spans almost 80 years: early childhood in pre-war Berlin, Switzerland and Paris; teenage years in London; then training at the Central School of Arts and Crafts just after the war, where Kerr devoted most of her energy to painting, consequently failing her diploma in book illustration. It was not until twenty years later, as a mother of young children, that her thoughts turned to picture books.

The Tiger Who Came to Tea was a bedtime story that Kerr had told time and again for her daughter, so turning it into a picture book text was quite easy.

'So the tiger came into the kitchen and sat down at the table.' Final artwork

The tiger developed from sketches she had made at the zoo, and her own kitchen provided the cupboards and the tea table. Had Kerr been working a few years earlier, it might have been difficult to accurately reproduce the vivid coloured inks which are such a memorable feature of the work, but with full-colour reproduction by then the norm, the way was clear. Together with *Mog the Forgetful Cat* (1970), *The Tiger Who Came to Tea* claims the unusual distinction (for a picture book) of being in print continuously for over 40 years.

That Kerr was destined to become an author and illustrator seems evident from the pictures and stories that she created as a child, which her mother miraculously kept safe as the family moved from place to place after fleeing Nazi Germany in 1933. The pictures – street scenes, school days, summertime at the beach – are full of narrative incident, with no hint of trauma or upheaval: an unselfconscious child's eye view of events and experiences which Kerr later described in her semi-autobiographical novel *When Hitler Stole Pink Rabbit* (1971).

Top: *'And then he looked round the kitchen to see what else he could find.'* Final artwork

In her native Germany, where *When Hitler Stole Pink Rabbit* has become a staple classroom text, Kerr is better known as an author than as an illustrator. Yet, partly in deference to her father Alfred Kerr, husband Nigel Kneale, and son, Matthew Kneale – all highly acclaimed writers – Kerr always describes herself as an illustrator, first and foremost. However, as her childhood creations suggest, being an illustrator is not just about being able to draw; an instinct for storytelling and a sense of humour are just as important.

'A good example of how much a make-believe situation gains from matter-of-fact treatment. Strong on domestic detail, an engaging, easily grasped story, charming illustrations which dovetail particularly well with the text.'

Miriam Goss reviewing *The Tiger Who Came to Tea*, *Observer*, December 1968.

Top: *'The burglar said, "Bother that cat!"'*
Final artwork from *Mog the Forgetful Cat* (1970)

A fairground in Germany, c.1933.
The very oldest drawings in Kerr's
archive date from before the family
fled Berlin; this scene was probably
inspired by a visit to a Harvest Festival.
Kerr recalls drawing the three children
on the slide, all in different positions

'I can't remember a time when I didn't want to draw.
It seemed a normal way to pass one's time, just as
it was normal for my brother Michael to kick a ball
about. I liked to draw figures in motion, and
I always drew them from the feet up, which
I would now find difficult.'

Judith Kerr, *Judith Kerr's Creatures*, London:
HarperCollins Children's Books, 2013, p. 8.

School-room,
Switzerland,1933.
This drawing was made in
Switzerland, where the family
lived for about six months
during 1933. In *When Hitler
Stole Pink Rabbit* (1971), Kerr
describes the village school
with characteristic dead-pan
humour: 'though Herr Graupe
was not a very good teacher of
more conventional subjects he
was a remarkable yodeller.'

" Il me faudrait au moins cinq chouffleurs comme ça pour mes petits-enfants ! "

*'I will need at least five
cauliflowers like that one for
my grandchildren.'* 1935.
This image shows Kerr's
grandmother, who lived in
Nice, buying vegetables at a
market stall, in preparation
for a visit by Kerr and her
brother. It was a family joke
that the children both had
large appetites

The Stone Book Quartet

by Alan Garner *(William Collins Sons & Co Ltd, 1976–1978)*

MICHAEL FOREMAN *Born 1938*

It is not unusual for author and illustrator to communicate only through an editor. *The Stone Book* and its three sequels are notable exceptions to the rule.

Foreman's response to Garner's text for *The Stone Book* was to work in etching: an unusually old-fashioned choice, but one that reflected an important theme of the narrative – the skill of the craftsman. After seeing sample etchings, Garner declared them 'magnificently bold … a landmark'.

Nevertheless, he urged the illustrator to come to Cheshire where the story was set:

Facing page: cover designs for the first editions of all four titles in the Quartet, published by Collins between 1976 and 1978

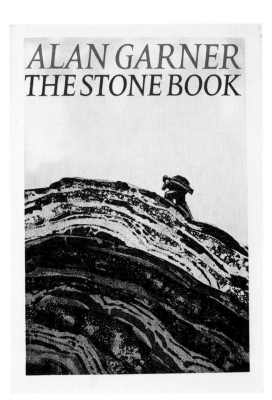

ALAN GARNER
THE STONE BOOK

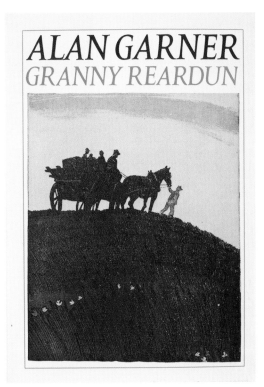

ALAN GARNER
GRANNY REARDUN

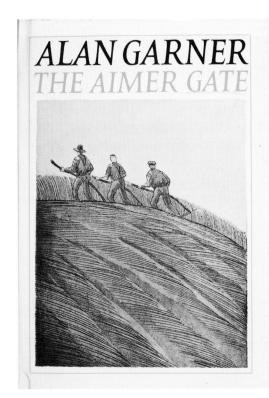

ALAN GARNER
THE AIMER GATE

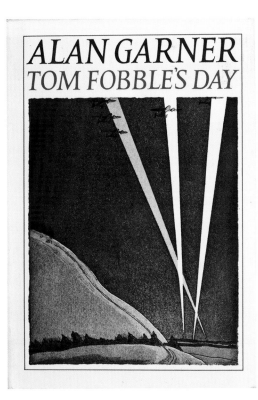

ALAN GARNER
TOM FOBBLE'S DAY

'it will be even better if you can come here for yourself and experience the ground', not least because what had started as a single story was turning into a quartet featuring successive generations of Garner's family.

Foreman duly visited Garner at home. He later commented that, had he known that there would be four titles instead of just one, he might have employed a less labour-intensive medium.

To ensure that Foreman's illustrations could be accurate in every detail, Garner gave him photographs, a book about fossils, and even an extract from an old ironworker's catalogue.

On the picture of William visiting Grandad in his blacksmith's workshop in *Tom Fobble's Day*, Garner asked for several changes. Two holes were missing from the anvil; strips of paper should be taped across the windows to protect against bomb-blast and William needed a gas mask canister on his back and clogs in place of shoes (Garner's wife Griselda supplied a drawing to show what these should look like).

Instead of making a new plate, Foreman made the alterations in pen, on the printed artwork. This was possible because the illustrations were reproduced photographically, not printed direct from the plate, as would have been the case in the nineteenth century. The plate and the print in the Seven Stories collection show the image in its uncorrected state.

The medium of etching gives Foreman's illustrations a powerful, elemental quality. When the stories were later re-issued in paperback, he was commissioned to re-create the images as line-drawings. While the content remained the same, the use of dense cross-hatching in place of smooth inky blackness created a very different effect.

Top: the etching plate (left); the printed image in the first edition (centre); and the re-drawn image in the 1979 paperback edition (right)

Facing page: *'Under the grating was the bench where Grandad sat.'* The image as it appears in the original etching

The Little Books

(Jonathan Cape, 1974–1975)

JOHN BURNINGHAM *Born 1936*

John Burningham's Little Books were inspired by first-hand observation of his own young children and their friends. Small and square-ish, each opening has a single sentence on the left hand page (no punctuation) and a picture on the right. It would be easy to underestimate the level of sophistication of these miniature works of art.

As in all of Burningham's work, the narrative is shared between the words and the pictures. Whether playing with a friend, a dog or a pet rabbit, emptying the kitchen cupboard or having fun in the snow, the young protagonist enjoys the simplest pleasures of childhood.

Facing page: *'fed the ducks'.* Artwork for unpublished title, *The Park* (c.1975)

> 'How difficult it is to hit exactly the right
> pitch with simple books for the very young:
> how unerringly John Burningham
> does just this.'

Elaine Moss, *Children's Books of the Year*, 1975,
London: Hamish Hamilton, 1976, p. 18.

Top left: *'smelt the flowers'*. Artwork for unpublished title,
The Park (c.1975)

Top right: *'And he peed on the flowers'*. Illustration from
The Dog (1975)

Left: *'I would like him to stay in the garden but he eats
Daddy's plants'*. Unpublished artwork for *The Rabbit* (1974)

THE PARK

There is lightness and humour, but also an emotional truth that makes the books a good read for parents as well as children, although Burningham's Dog peeing on the flowers provoked controversy in some quarters!

Eight Little Books were published between 1974 and 1975, and at least two other titles (*The Park* and *The Seaside*) were envisaged but never reached fruition. The Seven Stories archive includes work for the unpublished titles, plus unused images from the published books, which reveal the range of techniques involved in producing even the simplest image. Working on sheets of fine pen board, cut to size, Burningham outlines his figures in reddish-brown ink, over a light pencil sketch. The colours are a mixture of wax crayon, coloured pencil and coloured inks, applied with both pen and brush; here and there he scratches lines into the surface of the board to add texture. Mistakes are sometimes corrected by scraping away larger patches of the surface – an old illustrator's trick – but more often he simply discards the images which don't work and starts again. Drawing directly onto board in this way means that there is no loss of freshness or spontaneity in the transition from preparatory to finished artwork.

Rabbit & Pork, Rhyming Talk

(Hamish Hamilton, 1975)

JOHN LAWRENCE *Born 1933*

John Lawrence is one of very few illustrators of children's books to specialise in wood engraving, having trained under Gertrude Hermes at London's Central School in the mid-1950s. He has always been excited by the engraving process: the mysterious tools, the blocks, the mark-making – sparks on a black surface – and the magical moment when the paper comes off the press and a negative image appears on the paper.

For a long time, however, most of Lawrence's commissions were for line drawings; a great admirer of Ardizzone, he is a master of pen and ink in his own right.

© Cambridge News

Facing page: cover artwork. Hand-drawn dummy (above) and the published version (below)

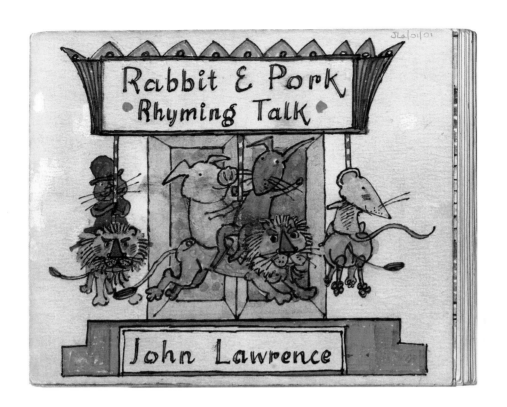

Brightly coloured image from the dummy

'All Afloat: Coat'. Final artwork, wood engraved

It was not until he had worked with editor Julia MacRae for a number of years that Lawrence was able to secure a commission for his first entirely wood-engraved picture book: *Rabbit and Pork*. The text, based on Cockney rhyming slang, is a sequence of verses linked together into a humorous but somewhat elusive narrative.

An ambitious venture, the book was not a commercial success, but was widely admired by wood engravers and led to a number of prestigious commissions. Lawrence's colourful dummy for *Rabbit and Pork* is now held at Seven Stories, alongside some of the prints – highlighting the dramatic transition from drawn to engraved image.

Since around 2000, Lawrence has worked mainly on engravings for texts by other authors, both picture books and longer works of poetry and prose. He now uses vinyl rather than wood for most of his engraving, mainly because it is so much cheaper.

He still prints the images himself, using an old Albion press in the corner of his workroom, but he also uses computer software to join images together, to add colour and create composites; he likes to imagine the Albion and the Apple Mac talking to one another after the lights have been turned out.

Working in a completely different style: hand-drawn final artwork for *The Christmas Cat* (1991) by Robert Westall, published by Methuen

Jackdaw & Rook: Book

Butcher's Hook : Look

Endpaper design from the dummy of *Rabbit and Pork*

The Most Amazing Hide-and-Seek Alphabet Book *(Kestrel Books, 1977)*

ROBERT CROWTHER *Born 1948*

Robert Crowther created the first version of his pop-up alphabet book while studying for an MA at the Royal College of Art. The roughs were drawn in felt pen on cartridge paper, but even at this early stage the paper engineering was carefully worked out. A full-scale dummy – entitled *The Magic Alphabet* – was the final outcome of the project. After graduating, Crowther had some difficulty finding a publisher, because the 26 pop-ups – one for each letter of the alphabet – made it difficult and costly to produce.

Facing page: cover designs. Dummy version (above) and first edition (below)

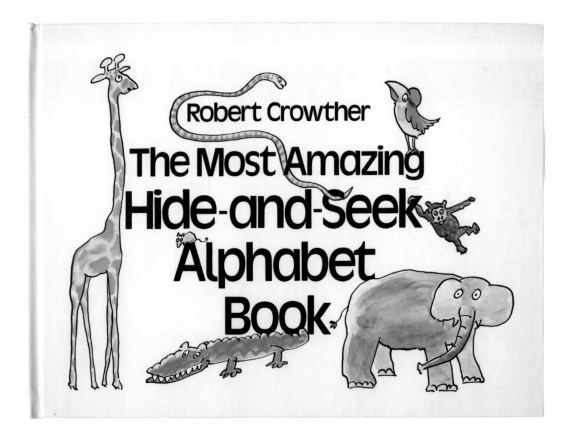

The Magic Alphabet

Robert Crowther

The Most Amazing Hide-and-Seek Alphabet Book

Once it was finally published, the book quickly became a bestseller and is still in print today. Meanwhile Crowther has gone on to produce numerous original and inventive pop-up books for both young and older children.

Pop-up books are often termed 'novelties', which tends to undermine their educational value, though the use of moveable elements to explain difficult concepts can be traced as far back as the Middle Ages.

Most of the moveable parts in Crowther's alphabet book are not, strictly speaking, 'pop-ups' at all – since, instead of springing up when the page is turned, they involve the reader in pulling a lever or a tab to create an effect. His devices exploit the shape of the letters, using humour and surprise to engage the young reader: an ape dangles from the low hanging 'branch' of the letter 'a', a sleepy owl stares out from the hollow letter 'o' and a curly snake uncoils when the letter 's' is folded back.

Some of Crowther's first ideas didn't make the final version. For example, his 'u' for urial (a wild sheep found in Central Asia) was (not surprisingly) replaced by an umbrella bird. Most of the paper engineering, however, was faithfully reproduced. The original layout sheets – complete with hand-drawn animals – show the complicated and detailed planning needed to ensure that every piece is precision-made for perfect operation, time after time.

Top: 'A is for ape'. Trial (left) and printed version (right)

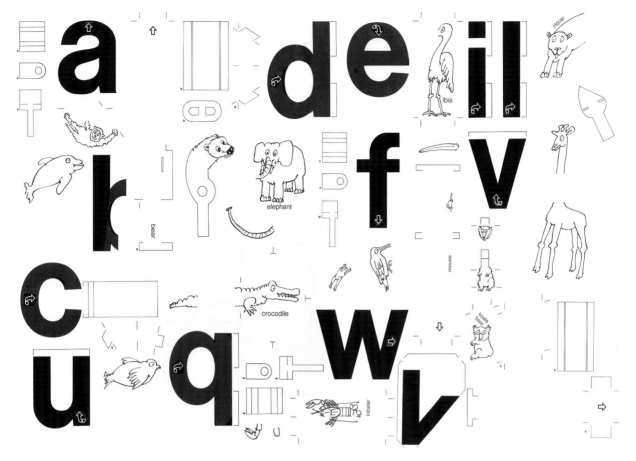

One of a set of hand-drawn layout sheets for *The Most Amazing Hide-and-Seek Alphabet Book* with flat outlines for all of the pieces required to create the pop-up mechanisms for each letter

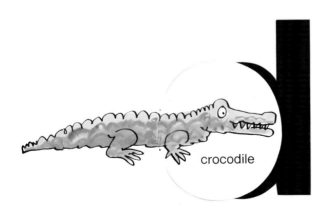

'It could well be argued that this was the breakthrough movable book in the British market, in terms of both its originality and the daring scale of its production.'

Geoff Fox, 'Movable Books',
in Kimberley Reynolds and Nicholas Tucker (eds.)
Children's Publishing in Britain Since 1945,
Aldershot: Scolar Press, 1997, pp. 86–109.

Above: detail from the dummy. When closed, only the letter forms are visible; when a flap is lifted, an animal appears – in this case, a crocodile

Sunshine (Kestrel, 1981)

JAN ORMEROD *1946–2013*

Courtesy of Laura Ormerod

Sunshine is a completely wordless picture book, telling the story of the first hour or so of a little girl's day, from waking up with the sun to leaving the house with mum for school. It is a deceptively simple concept. Ormerod's preparatory work reveals how she drew on her minute observations of ordinary family life to construct a story, then used colour and compositional devices to give it shape.

A storyboard with images roughly drawn in irregularly shaped rectangles shows that, from the outset, Ormerod envisaged using frames of different sizes to vary the pace of the narrative – inspired by her avid reading of comics as a child.

66 Facing page: early storyboard, including ideas that never made it into the published version

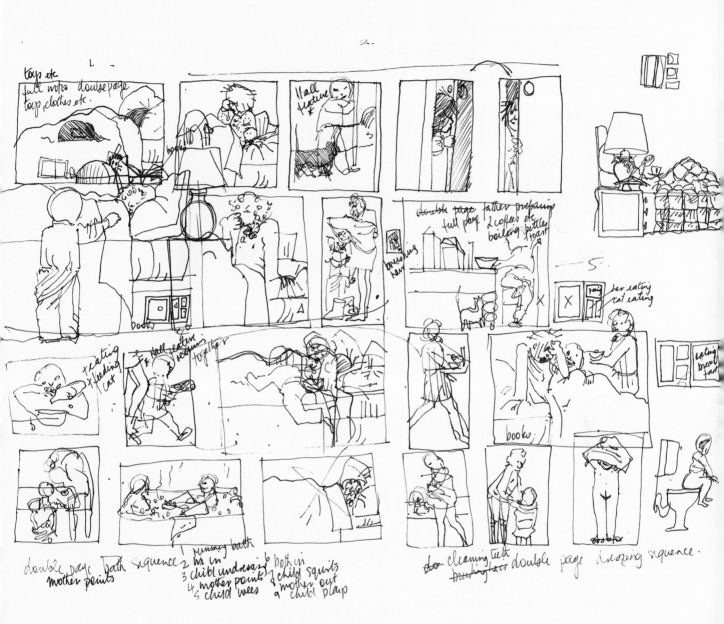

Some key images – the girl waking up, rubbing her eyes, and peeping through her parents' door – make it to the final version; others, including the cat and the scene of mother and daughter in the bath, disappear along the way. The dramatic double-page spread in which Dad burns the toast is completely missing from this early sequence.

Ormerod exploits the luminosity of watercolour on white paper with great effect to communicate the changing light of early morning. This is particularly clear from the first six frames, in which the bedroom becomes gradually brighter as the sun rises; different versions of the picture in which the girl is shown sitting up in bed with a book demonstrate that Ormerod worked hard to establish the colour and tonality. In the toast-burning sequence the effect is reversed – the space round Dad's head becoming gradually darker until he finally realises what is happening.

Jan Ormerod grew up and trained in Western Australia, but moved to England in 1980. *Sunshine* was her first picture book; it won the 1982 Mother Goose Award, given annually to 'the most exciting newcomer to British children's book illustration', and was also highly commended for the Kate Greenaway Medal.

Top: going in to see Mum and Dad. Final artwork

'My task as a visual storyteller is to observe, record, and edit. Some images go straight from life into a book. Most need to be carefully sifted, reinvented, reorganized.'

Jan Ormerod, 'In Her Own Words', www.harpercollins.com/authors.

Reading in bed. Preliminary artwork, experimenting with a different colour palette

Waking up. Final artwork for the opening sequence of images

1 Hunter (Bodley Head, 1985)

PAT HUTCHINS *Born 1942*

© Morgan Hutchins

1 *Hunter* is a counting book, in which one comical-looking hunter marches determinedly ahead, oblivious to the growing number of animals emerging from the undergrowth behind him: two elephants, three giraffes, four ostriches … and finally ten parrots. At the end of the book the hunter turns round to find all the animals staring at him, and runs away in a panic. Hutchins had already used a similar formula to great effect in her hugely successful first picture book, *Rosie's Walk* (1968).

Facing page: *'3 giraffes'*. An early experiment with gouache

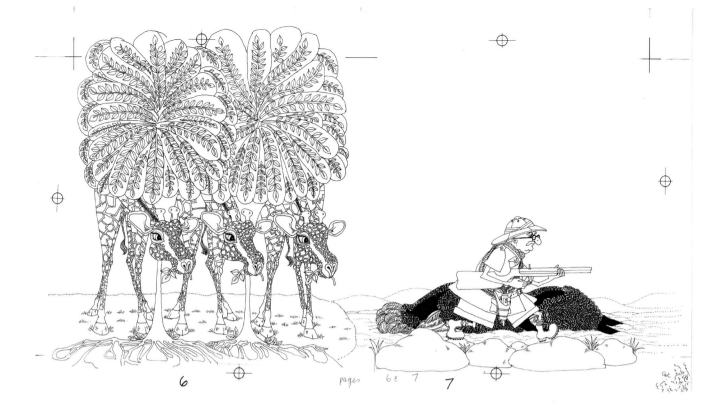

6

pages 6 & 7

7

 giraffes

'Pat Hutchins's unique combination of strong colour and memorable patterning has never been used to better effect.'

Margery Fisher, *The Sunday Times*, c.1985.

The creation of the artwork involved a number of false starts. First, Hutchins experimented with collage, but quickly lost patience with cutting and sticking, and tried gouache on board instead. This resulted in a luscious frieze-like image of the three giraffes, but Hutchins felt that the lack of a clear outline and the rich variety of tones made the picture more difficult to read.

Finally, she reverted to black line and colour separations. In those days most illustrators were familiar with the process of preparing work for colour reproduction by separating it into its constituent primary colours. This involves drawing a key image on white paper, then a series of further drawings on layers of semi-transparent overlay – one for each colour of printing ink to be used. So, for each spread, Hutchins drew an outline in black ink, and painted four overlays for the black, blue, red and yellow inks that would be combined in the finished work. This means there is no 'original' colour artwork. Hutchins had to work out how to achieve the final image by combining the different colours – blue and yellow producing green, for example. Each sheet has registration marks in the margin, enabling the printer to position the different layers exactly.

There are just sixteen spreads in *1 Hunter*, including the title page and book jacket, but for each of these there is a key drawing and four overlays: no fewer than 80 sheets in total.

Facing page: *'3 giraffes'*. Key line drawing (above) and final printed version (below)

This page: cover design, first edition

Angelina Ballerina
by Katharine Holabird *(Aurum Press, 1983)*

HELEN CRAIG *Born 1934*

When Katharine Holabird and Helen Craig collaborated on *Angelina Ballerina* they had no idea that the book would grow into a whole series. Craig had drawn dancing mice before, but this was her first opportunity to create a fully developed character. There have now been 23 Angelina picture books, numerous spin-off publications, animations, merchandise and even a real ballet; quite an achievement for a hand-drawn mouse.

Author and illustrator have both donated their Angelina archives to Seven Stories,

Facing page: '*"Oh Angelina, your dancing is nothing but a nuisance!" exclaimed her mother.*'
Colour rough (above) and final artwork (below)

Above: *'They all practised curtsies and pliés and ran around the room together just like fairies.'* Final artwork (top) and progressive roughs in black and white (below left) and in colour (below right)

Angelina Ballerina

Illustrations by Helen Craig Text by Katharine Holabird

providing a fascinating record of how the series has developed and endured. Craig's drafts for *Angelina Ballerina* – her first full-scale picture book – reveal how she approached characterisation, expression and movement (*how does a mouse curtsey?*).

Every intricate detail of the setting is carefully worked out: the country cottage where the family lives; the ballet school with its mirrored walls; and the spectacular Mouseland theatre, where each tiny character – whether on stage, in the orchestra, seated in the stalls, or even waiting to selling ice creams during the interval – has a distinct personality.

Not surprisingly, for each image there are several progressive roughs – more than a hundred in total for the book – first in pencil, then ink, each one more finished than the last. Craig often dates her drafts, sometimes adding notes to herself: 'Ideal of illustration – half atmosphere – half

information. Total information – interests but does not excite. Total atmosphere – ie impressionistic illustration – excites for a moment but loses interest quickly.'

Craig's commitment to using pictorial information to draw out the humour in Holabird's narrative, and to hold the interest of the child reader through numerous re-readings, has been a key factor in Angelina's success. As the series progressed, Holabird and Craig talked about ideas for stories and settings that would offer not only new adventures for Angelina but also new opportunities for visual invention. Thus, Angelina goes ice skating and camping, travels on a canal boat, and even – in the latest book in the series – visits 'The Big Cheese' (aka New York).

Top: cover design, first edition

'At last she became the famous ballerina Mademoiselle Angelina, and people came from far and wide to enjoy her lovely dancing.'
The final scene in the book – the magnificent Mouseland theatre. Preparatory artwork (top) and final artwork (bottom)

with out coat of
arms.

Tog the Ribber or Granny's Tale

by Paul Coltman *(André Deutsch and Farrar Straus & Giroux, 1985)*

GILLIAN McCLURE *Born 1948*

Courtesy of Gillian McClure

T*og the Ribber* is a ghost story in verse, written by Gillian McClure's father, the poet Paul Coltman. The poem had been awarded a prize in a competition; Charles Causley praised 'the real invention of [the poem's] language' and Ted Hughes described it as 'an authentic tour de force'.

McClure's first illustrations for *Tog* were fairly conventional – pen and ink, tightly cross-hatched. After completing thirteen spreads, McClure stopped. Family life intervened, and by the time she resumed, her ideas had evolved, the old work was set aside and she started afresh.

Facing page: *'I shuddud in the glavering goom as homing through the only wood I skibbed and teetered past Tog's tomb.'* Final artwork with ghostly border decoration

Previously, McClure had seemed afraid to represent the terrifying figure of Tog. Now he is a skeletal figure with long bony fingers. With each verse, Tog becomes more threatening – bending down from the tree, reaching out to touch the little girl and finally chasing her through the woods.

McClure saw an opportunity to exploit the interplay between frame and image to imply the shifting border between fear and reality. As the terror grows to a climax, the illustrations break beyond the bounds of the frame, eventually spreading right across the page.

McClure adopted an unusual technique to create texture and depth: first applying a layer of masking fluid to form a waterproof skin on the surface of the board, then rubbing the mask with her finger to create tiny holes, and painting over it with a thin glaze of dilute acrylic to create a stippled effect. Further rubbing and pulling of the mask made bigger holes, which, when painted over, produced a lacy pattern. She could then work into the holes and the unmasked areas, creating plants and creatures which seem to emerge, ghost-like, from the background.

McClure's final illustrations were every bit as original and intense as her father's verse. The book was commended for the Kate Greenaway Medal, but was sadly not a commercial success – seemingly the market in the mid-1980s was not ready for a picture book for older children.

'I shrikked, "Oh woly, woly me!"
as Tog begun to clumber down.'
Final artwork

The Snow Queen

by Hans Christian Andersen,
translated by Naomi Lewis *(Walker Books, 1988)*

ANGELA BARRETT *Born 1955*

Angela Barrett's illustrations for *The Snow Queen* are both beautiful and profoundly melancholic – a fitting match for the brooding magic of Andersen's storytelling, in this version by the eminent writer and critic Naomi Lewis. The *Snow Queen* artwork donated by Barrett to Seven Stories provides some insights into how she approached the challenge of re-illustrating such a well-known text.

Barrett's haunting compositions emerge gradually from rough sketches: a mass of rapid pencil or pen lines builds shape and volume; important features, such as

Facing page: *'Little Kay was quite blue with cold.'*
Final artwork showing Kay and the Snow Queen
in her icy palace

The next set of roughs provides a map for the later drawings; some showing signs of having been traced in pencil from one to the other. Instead of a light box, Barrett tapes the roughs to the window and lays her watercolour paper over the top.

As you would expect in a fairy tale, every detail carries meaning. Sometimes this is a direct reflection of the text – hence, on a rough drawing of Kay and Gerda on the rooftop, Barrett has scribbled to herself: 'poor, don't forget'. Other times, the visual language works independently, using mysterious shadows and distorted perspective to create a sense of foreboding.

For her final artwork, Barrett uses dense layers of pencil, pastel, watercolour and gouache to create dramatic intensity; so, in the picture of the robbers' castle, where the distant reaches of the room have a velvety darkness, the reddish glow of the fire seems to warm the centre of the page.

faces, are picked out carefully as she tries to pin down the characterisation; a thin wash of pale watercolour establishes mood and tonality. Barrett's sketchbook becomes a collection of interconnected images, a place in which to 'jot down ideas on the spur of the moment … dreams, and other things that pass fleetingly through [her] mind' (interview with Joanna Carey in the catalogue accompanying *The Magic Pencil* exhibition, organized by the British Council, 2002).

This page: *'Gerda couldn't even close her eyes, not knowing whether she was to live or die.'* Final artwork showing Gerda and the robber girl in the robbers' castle

Facing page: Loose sketch of Gerda and the raven (above) and pages from Barrett's sketchbook showing early versions of various images, including the robbers' castle (below)

*'Angela Barrett's pictures are
so cold and frosty the paper positively crackles…
All schools should buy several copies.'*

Pam Harwood, *Books For Keeps*, January 1992.

1990–2013

'At the present time, artists trained in the formal disciplines
of drawing and design are working alongside people who,
although they might seem less well equipped in these traditional
skills, are overflowing with exuberant, sophisticated and
ever-inventive approaches to book illustration.'

Martin Salisbury, *Illustrating Children's Books*, A & C Black, 2004, p. 16.

Facing page: *'There she met a boy as big as her finger.'* Final artwork by Bob Graham
for *Jethro Byrde, Fairy Child* (2002). Top: cover design, first edition

Billy and Belle *(Reinhardt Books, 1992)*

SARAH GARLAND *Born 1944*

Sarah Garland trained as a typographer at the London College of Printing, but began illustrating in the mid-1960s. Her picture books for young children brilliantly capture the happy muddle of family life with small children and pets. The stories are sparked by her observations of people and events; she travels everywhere with a pencil and a handy sketchbook. As words and pictures gradually coalesce, she works through the stages of storyboarding and layout, using a rough dummy for reference.

For her final artwork she uses pen and watercolour, but aims to keep the lines as lively and fluid as in the sketches.

Facing page: cover design from an early and very rough dummy showing that Belle was originally going to be named Pearl, after the little girl Garland had been drawing. She decided to change the name to protect the family's privacy

Billy and Pearl

Sarah Garland

Joyce

For *Billy and Belle*, Garland spent two days sketching at a primary school in London and at the house of some friends, on whom the main characters are based. The story is about the day that a new baby is born: Mum and Dad have to go to the hospital, so little Belle goes with her brother Billy to school, for the first time ever. Unfortunately it is 'bring your pet to school day', and when Belle loses her spider, chaos ensues.

Garland's portrayal of a family with parents of different races proved unexpectedly controversial. She was asked to change the endpaper illustrations, which show the parents in bed together, because sales and marketing departments said it would be difficult to secure co-editions of the book in South Africa, in the southern states of the USA and even in Scandinavia and France.

Garland refused to change the pictures and the book was eventually published just as she had drawn it. Unfortunately the gloomy predictions were accurate and the book went out of print for a time, but it has subsequently been re-issued by Frances Lincoln Children's Books.

Over the years, Garland has received many letters from families like the one in *Billy and Belle*, which have made her glad that she stuck to her original vision.

This page: pencil drawings from Garland's sketchbook

Facing page: final endpaper artwork (above) and cover design for the 2004 edition by Frances Lincoln Children's Books (below)

'I was just trying to show things as they are.
I go to London and sit in cafes or on buses and draw
and draw, so, of course, I see all races. In one book
I used a mixed race family because I have friends
who are. It wasn't meant to be an issue.'

Sarah Garland, interviewed by Julia Eccleshare,
Books For Keeps, No. 98, May 1996.

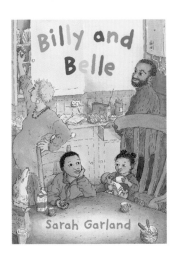

Floss *(Walker Books, 1993)*

KIM LEWIS *Born 1951*

Kim Lewis was brought up in Montreal, but Northumberland is her adopted home and the setting for her picture books. She moved there from London, with her husband, to run a sheep farm. Her books are full of detailed observations of the life and landscape all around her; she wanted rural children to have stories that reflected their experiences, and city children to have an insight into a very different way of living.

Lewis's first two picture books were made for her son (*The Shepherd Boy*, 1991) and daughter (*Emma's Lamb*, 1992). *Floss*, her third book, is about a football-loving sheepdog who comes from the city to work on the farm.

Facing page: *'She worked very hard to become a good sheepdog.'* Final artwork

'The transformation of Floss from family pet to sheep dog unfolds beautifully with Kim Lewis' evocative illustrations and deliberately spare text … warmth, simplicity and total lack of sentimentality.'

Judith Sharman reviewing *Floss*, *Books for Keeps*, No. 84, January 1994.

Early drafts of the text show that the themes of moving from city to country, remembering instinct, being torn between will and obedience, and achieving a balance between work and play were all in her mind from the outset, as was the basic structure of twelve sections for the twelve double spreads of a picture book. Nevertheless, Lewis struggled to establish the narratorial voice and it took nearly 30 re-workings before she was content.

Once the text was settled, the book seems to have taken shape visually with much less difficulty. Key images, such as the terraced streets on the first spread and 'sheep everywhere' at the dramatic climax of the story on the eighth spread, can be seen in the storyboard. From here, Lewis progressed through pencil sketches, establishing the content of each image in

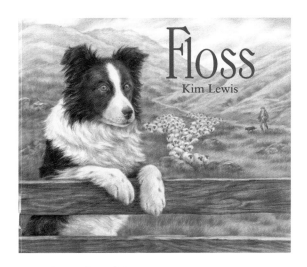

Cover design, first edition

more and more detail, before eventually switching to coloured pencil to create final artwork which brilliantly evokes the feel of wind on the rough grass and heather of the Northumberland hills, 'where nothing much grew except sheep'.

Facing page: storyboard; the layout here is close to the final version

Top left: '"*FLOSS! LIE DOWN!*"' Pencil sketch. Compare this to the corresponding image in the storyboard (spread eight)

'Floss did her best springs in the air.' Final artwork for the joyous last spread in the book

Jethro Byrde, Fairy Child

(Walker Books, 2002)

BOB GRAHAM *Born 1942*

© Walker Books

Bob Graham is an Australian illustrator who has spent many years working in England. He is known for the warmth of his stories about children and families in ordinary settings and situations.

In *Jethro Byrde, Fairy Child*, little Annabelle befriends a family of fairies amid the weeds and concrete in her backyard. The book won the 2002 Kate Greenaway Medal for the best illustrated book published in the UK.

Facing page: '*"We must go," Offin said at last.*' The fairy family prepares to depart through the gap in the fence. Final artwork

'I have no method; I just scratch away with my pen at the
surface of things, turn rocks over with my toe and sometimes
a potential story scuttles away like a crab.'

Bob Graham, quoted in 'Background on Bob Graham and Jethro Byrde Fairy Child',
July 2003, www.carnegiegreenaway.org.uk/pressdesk.

Annabelle spent a lot of her time in the back yard, especially the bit near the hole in the fence, where the weeds poked through and where the tiny tree forced its way up through the crack in the concrete.

Her dad read the newspaper down there and people put out their washing, and most days Annabelle brought The Family with her; three wooden dolls, a blue pig, a plastic railway porter, a running hare and two pottery chickens.

Graham's archive for *Jethro Byrde* is an unusually complete record of the process of creating a picture book. It comprises not just each draft and redraft of text and images but also letters, emails and other commentary recording the interactions between Graham and his editor and designer at Walker Books. This aspect of the creative process is easily overlooked, because the evidence for it generally vanishes when the book is finished.

While the heart of Graham's story remains constant, everything else is pulled about and changed, at least partly in response to editorial advice. He seems to have worked on text and images simultaneously, the book evolving as an integrated whole rather than in methodical stages. In his first drafts, key features of the setting and the characters and the contrast in size between human and fairy are all clearly established, but the narrative is more complicated, with several subplots which were dropped as the book progressed. There were at least five dummy books, each closer to the final version, as the story became more focused. The rough drawings were in blue pencil (which does not show up so much when copied) and ink, often on scraps of thin paper which could be pasted into a dummy. For the final artwork Graham worked with washes of brilliant watercolour. Even at this stage, at least one picture had to be changed: when the human hands proffering a plate of cakes looked (according to the designer) 'too fleshy and enormous', Graham redrew the image without them.

Facing page: *'Annabelle's mum bought fairy cakes and camomile tea in fairy cups.'* This final artwork had to be re-drawn without the hands

This page: double spread from first draft. Annabelle's 'Family' disappear from later drafts

Starring Tracy Beaker

by Jacqueline Wilson *(Doubleday, 2006)*

NICK SHARRATT *Born 1962*

Nick Sharratt has illustrated many picture books both on his own account and with other authors, but is probably still best-known for his long collaboration with Jacqueline Wilson, and especially for creating the visual identity of her most famous character, Tracy Beaker.

Though Wilson and Sharratt have become great friends, they still work entirely separately. The publisher sends a copy of Wilson's manuscript to Sharratt, who marks it up with ideas for illustrations. Almost every page has at least one graphic element, and some of the text is carried in handwritten lettering or speech bubbles – Sharratt's illustrations become an integral part of the storytelling.

Facing page: cover design, early rough

 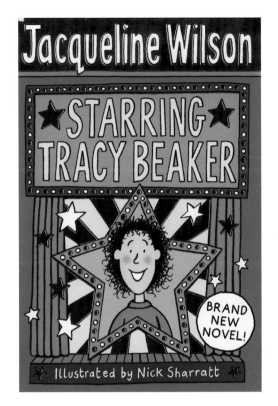

Tracy wears her heart on her sleeve, and the drawings map each stage in her emotional journey: ecstatic joy at being chosen to play Scrooge in the school production of *A Christmas Carol*; extreme anger when the headteacher threatens to take away the role; lump-in-throat sadness when her mum fails to turn up to see the play; and, finally, loving affection for her foster-mother Cam, who saves Christmas Day.

Sharratt works in a traditional way, progressing from pencil sketches through to successive ink revisions, drawing on thin, smooth paper, and using a lightbox to transfer from rough to finished artwork. Consistency is important: any figure that is not instantly recognisable is discarded and re-drawn. Having left art school in 1984, Sharratt belongs to perhaps the last generation of illustrators to have trained without computers: though he now uses Photoshop to add colour, the rest of the work is done entirely by hand. The final drawings are neatly set out on A4 sheets and numbered so that the book designer knows where to place them.

Top: cover designs. Colour rough (left) and first edition (right)

Top: final artwork – various drawings, on one sheet. At the top left is a drawing that went wrong and had to be started again

Sharratt's partnership with Jacqueline Wilson has shown that there is still a role for illustration in novels for children. It is simply impossible to imagine Wilson's novels being issued without Sharratt's illustrations – or indeed re-illustrated by another artist.

Above: *'That night I laboured long and hard over a big card. I drew the Dumping Ground and all of us guys outside, armed with dusters and brushes and maps.'*
Final artwork minus shading, which was added digitally later

107

Greek Hero *(Frances Lincoln Children's Books, 2007)*

MICK MANNING AND
BRITA GRANSTRÖM *Born 1959 & 1969*

Mick Manning and Brita Granström are both illustrators. They have been making non-fiction picture books together since 1996, and have received numerous awards for their creative contributions to an often-neglected aspect of children's reading.

The *Greek Hero* archive documents the tricky work of combining factual accuracy and engaging narrative. A consultant provided expert advice on the historical detail, but the development of the characters and storyline was led by Manning and Granström. After combing the National Curriculum and visiting the British Museum, they chose topics –

Facing page: *'Today is Ambrosia's wedding day!'.*
Final artwork

Greeks roughs revised 6/7/06 5:50 PM Page 24

The wedding guest sing loudly:
All alone a sweet apple reddens on the topmost branch... the apple pickers didn't notice it... they could not reach it!

Wedding

Ambrosia thinks Athena must have listened to her prayer. Today is her wedding day!
There was a great feast at her father's house. Now it's time for the procession to their new home.

Put more in

They all wear 'crowns of laurel leaves.

Torches to lead the way

nuts and ... to shower the wedding couple with

wedding gifts.

Few Ancient Greek wedding songs remain, so the example above – written by Sappho, a famous woman poet – is very important to historians.

Wedding celebrations lasted three days with lots of ceremonies such as the bride giving her old toys to the gods.

The wedding day began with a bath for the bride. After the feast her father gave her to the husband.

The couple travelled by chariot to the bride's new home, followed by their families, well-wishers and song.

24   25

Pencil rough for wedding scene, scanned and overlaid with text.
Note the annotation, 'cart not chariot + mules' and compare with the final artwork on the previous page. Evidently, Ambrosia's wedding transport was downgraded in response to this feedback

CART NOT CHARIOT + MULES

'The big issue is women again – as always we try to find a women's role model. In Greece they weren't allowed to do much, but I'm hoping we will be allowed to get away with what I have done.'

Mick Manning, writing to Gemma Rochelle at Frances Lincoln Children's Books. Email accompanying first draft of text, February 2006.
From the Mick Manning and Brita Granström collection at Seven Stories.

including the Greek gods, Athens, Sparta and the Olympic Games – then created a cast of characters and an episodic narrative.

Manning's email correspondence with the book's editor records several challenges that had to be resolved. Pinpointing an exact date for the story was important for the purposes of convincing 'fly on the wall' reportage, but with so much Greek history to choose from, it was not immediately obvious what the date should be. Starting with victory over the Persians in 479 BC meant that the story could take place in peacetime; this increased the opportunities to feature women, who were largely absent from public life in Ancient Greece. However, neither the iconic Parthenon at Athens nor the great Temple of Zeus at Olympia were built until after 479 BC, so they could not feature in the pictures.

The potter in his workshop. Pencil rough

Manning wanted the lead female character to accompany her husband to the Olympic Games, but this was vetoed by the consultant, as women were strictly forbidden: 'while this makes for a nice story, it is more important to give your young readers a correct idea of Greek society'. So Ambrosia stays at home, while Agathon competes in the athletics.

Granström's expressive pencil line, lucid watercolour and lively handwritten annotations convey a sense of movement, as though the characters were indeed drawn from life. Some unconventional collage materials underline the connections between past and present: a scrap of wool, some bay leaves and two wasps – the only insects in the whole of the Seven Stories Collection.

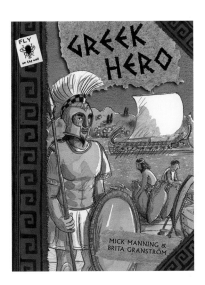

Cover design, first edition

My Dad's a Birdman
by David Almond *(Walker Books, 2007)*

POLLY DUNBAR *Born 1977*

© Walker Books

My Dad's a Birdman is about the re-discovery of joy and hope, and an extraordinary competition to fly across the River Tyne. The story originated as a play, which Almond wrote for the Young Vic in 2003. The characters remained with him, so he decided to adapt the story into a short novel for children aged around eight. He wanted it to have illustrations — too often missing from books for children of that age, who generally still want pictures, but feel they are too old for picture books.

Facing page: *'They started doing a bird dance round the table.'* Final artwork

'He reached into his pocket and found a worm. He held it up and let it dangle from his fingers, then he gobbled it up.' Pencil rough (above) and final artwork (right)

Though each admired the other's work, Almond and Dunbar did not meet until after *My Dad's a Birdman* was published. Almond was delighted when his editor at Walker Books, David Lloyd, proposed Dunbar as illustrator, but he had no wish to influence how the illustrations would develop, leaving everything to Dunbar and the team at Walker.

Happily, Dunbar responded intuitively to Almond's tender portrayal of the relationship between young Lizzie and her bereaved Dad, the pictures seeming to flow naturally onto the page. This is not always the case – sometimes she has to draw a character a hundred times before it 'comes to life'.

Before long, Dunbar had filled four sketchbooks with pencil drawings, and a fifth with rough layouts. To keep the freshness and immediacy of first response, she scanned her best sketches into the computer, cleaned up the lines, then printed them onto watercolour paper, before adding colour and collage; the collage creates a textured effect which reflects the significance of feathers in the story.

Almond and Dunbar collaborated again on *The Boy who Climbed into the Moon* (2010). Although they knew each other by this time, they chose not to meet or discuss the book beforehand, both agreeing that it is better when 'the life between the words and pictures just happens'.

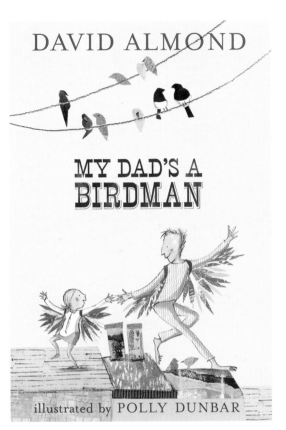

Above: cover design, first edition
Right: pencil drawings of Dad and Lizzie

Time for Bed, Fred! (Bloomsbury, 2013)

YASMEEN ISMAIL *Born 1981*

Yasmeen Ismail graduated from art school in her native Dublin in 2002 and spent ten years running her own animation company before deciding that she really wanted to be an illustrator.

Happily, working in animation had developed invaluable skills that Ismail was able transfer to her first picture book, *Time for Bed, Fred!*; not just drawing for many hours every day, but also scripting, storyboarding and editing – often ruthlessly – to get the narrative right.

Facing page: some of Ismail's numerous quick sketches of Fred in various poses, with her annotations

Mummy along.
Can I use this?

in the tree.

out of bath

Early versions of Fred.
Unused artwork

Preparatory artwork. In the final composition, these clothes are arranged along a washing line

What is it Fred?

'*What is it Fred?*' Print-out of an
unused composite image

She drew endless roughs of Fred, experimenting with different colours, poses and expressions, until she was confident that she knew the character inside out. Her efforts paid off – in 2014, *Time for Bed, Fred!* won the V&A Illustration award in the category for book illustration.

Ismail's work is different from any other illustration in the Seven Stories Collection to date, because of the way she combines traditional brush and watercolour technique with the use of digital editing to create her final artwork.

The pictures in the book may look as though they have been produced in an entirely conventional way, but in fact they are all composite images: the individual elements – flowers, trees, household articles – are painted separately, scanned, then layered and positioned on-screen, giving Ismail complete control over every detail of each spread.

Ismail paints directly onto high quality watercolour paper, using her roughs for reference but without under-drawing, resulting in great vibrancy and directness. Even the clothes, which in the book are shown pegged along a washing line and spattered with mud, were all created separately (modelled on images in a mail order catalogue); the dirty dog and the mud (also painted) were scanned and layered on top afterwards. The final artwork, therefore, is a digital file, and the quality of scanner and screen are as important to the creative process as paint and paper.

Cover design, first edition

The very first Fred.
Unused artwork

the story of the archive

All of the stories in this book are drawn from the Seven Stories Collection – a unique national archive of manuscripts and artwork by leading British writers and illustrators for children. Spanning more than 80 years, from the 1930s to the present day, the Collection tells a story of dramatic change in children's books – as in so many other aspects of everyday life in Britain – while the sketches, scribbles, drafts and redrafts, notes and correspondence reveal a multitude of individual approaches to the creative process.

At the time of writing, the Seven Stories Collection includes work by around 200 writers and illustrators. Individual archives vary in size from single pieces of artwork to multi-layered holdings covering an entire working life.

Through the Magic Mirror:
The World of Anthony Browne.
Exhibition at Seven Stories, 2011

As the Collection grows, new connections and comparisons become possible, and richer, more complex histories of children's literature emerge than can be told from the printed books alone.

The Seven Stories visitor centre in Newcastle upon Tyne, the only museum in the country devoted solely to children's books, has welcomed around 70,000 visitors a year since it opened to the public in 2005. Our learning and participation programme reaches over 30,000 children and young people every year, and our touring exhibitions have travelled to museums and galleries nationwide. All of the illustrators included in this book have been exhibited by Seven Stories and/or featured in our learning programmes at some point in the last ten years.

This publication has been funded as part of 'Picture book in Progress', a project supported by Arts Council England to enable aspiring illustrators to encounter the original artwork in our Collection. The opportunity to look at sketches, roughs and other work in progress proved to be inspirational, giving students the confidence to experiment and take creative risks. It also gave them insights into the working world of illustration and the realities of collaboration with authors, editors and publishers.

As Seven Stories moves into its second decade, we want to continue building the Collection, acquiring more great work by authors and illustrators past and present, and enabling as many people as possible to enjoy and be inspired by it. If you would like to help us save, celebrate and share this wonderful heritage, please get in touch.

INFO@SEVENSTORIES.ORG.UK

WWW.SEVENSTORIES.ORG.UK

REGISTERED CHARITY NUMBER 1056812

Supported using public funding by
ARTS COUNCIL ENGLAND

© Seven Stories National Centre for Children's Books

'Children's books have found a home,
and what a home. Here is a place at Seven Stories
where children and their stories, where writers and illustrators,
poets and storytellers can come together to celebrate the best of
children's literature. Nowhere I've been is more likely to inspire
children, parents and teachers towards a love of books.'

Michael Morpurgo, in a letter to Kate Edwards, Chief Executive,
following a visit to Seven Stories in November, 2008.

All of the illustration in the Seven Stories Collection has been acquired though gifts of work or funding. Those who have generously supported the acquisitions featured in this book are listed here. We are always pleased to hear from other potential donors or supporters – please get in touch via the Seven Stories website (www.sevenstories.org.uk) or by email: collections@sevenstories.org.uk.

RUTH GERVIS'S illustrations for *Ballet Shoes* were purchased in 2000. Support from the Royal Literary Fund enabled this and other early acquisitions.

A large archive of work by **HAROLD JONES** was donated by Stephanie and Gabrielle Jones in 2005. Artwork for Jones's masterpiece *Lavender's Blue* was purchased with funding from The Art Fund and the ACE/V&A Purchase Fund in 2014.

EILEEN SOPER'S illustrations for *The Toys Come to Life* were purchased at auction in 2014, with funding from the Rackham Foundation.

Noddy illustrations by **HARMSEN VAN DER BEEK**, including his famous letter to Enid Blyton, were donated by members of the Blyton family at various times.

DOROTHY CRAIGIE'S artwork for *The Little Train* was donated by the late Dr Gerry Bell, in memory of his late wife Muriel Bell, an enthusiastic collector of Craigie's work.

Artwork for **EDWARD ARDIZZONE'S** *Tim in Danger* was donated by Christianna Clemence, Edward Ardizzone's daughter; *Tim and Charlotte* was donated by Antoinetta Ardizzone in memory of Nick Ardizzone. Artwork for *The Little Train* was purchased in 2011 with funding from the Friends of the National Libraries, MLA/V&A Purchase Grant Fund and the Art Fund.

Work by **SHIRLEY HUGHES** including the dummy for *Lucy and Tom's Day* has been deposited on long term loan by the illustrator.

ANTONY MAITLAND donated work for a number of titles including *Mrs Cockle's Cat* in 2007.

The **FAITH JAQUES** archive was purchased in 1998 with assistance from the Friends of the National Libraries.

JUDITH KERR deposited her wonderful archive in 2008.

MICHAEL FOREMAN gave his illustrations for *The Stone Book Quartet* in 2005.

JOHN BURNINGHAM gave his Little Books artwork in 2011.

JOHN LAWRENCE has donated work for a number of titles at various times, between 2000 and 2014.

ROBERT CROWTHER gave the work for three of his pop-up titles in 2006.

JAN ORMEROD donated her artwork for *Sunshine* in 2007, after some of it had been shown in our opening exhibition.

PAT HUTCHINS and her late husband Laurence Hutchins donated artwork for three books in 2005, one by Laurence and two by Pat.

HELEN CRAIG donated her entire Angelina archive in 2013.

GILLIAN MCCLURE gave the artwork for *Tog the Ribber* and four other books in 2009.

ANGELA BARRETT'S *Snow Queen* archive was donated by the illustrator in 2005.

SARAH GARLAND gave work for *Billy and Belle* and two other titles in 2010. Artwork by her mother, the illustrator Charlotte Hough, was donated to Seven Stories by Sarah's sister, Deborah Moggach, in 2009.

KIM LEWIS donated her work for eleven picture books, including *Floss*, in 2006.

BOB GRAHAM'S artwork for *Jethro Byrde, Fairy Child* was acquired by Seven Stories on a part-gift, part-purchase basis in 2009. The purchase was funded by a donation from Jan and Ron Clements to mark Jan's retirement from Seven Stories' Board of Trustees; the rest of the material was donated by Bob Graham.

NICK SHARRATT gave his work for *Starring Tracy Beaker* and another title by Jacqueline Wilson, *Best Friends*, in 2006.

MICK MANNING and **BRITA GRANSTRÖM** donated their *Greek Hero* archive in 2007.

POLLY DUNBAR'S illustrations for *My Dad's a Birdman* were acquired through a part-gift, part-purchase arrangement in 2008.

YASMEEN ISMAIL is one of our most recent supporters, donating the artwork for *Time for Bed, Fred!* plus other work, in 2013.

author's acknowledgements

Many people have helped with the development, design and production of this book. I would particularly like to thank Jacqueline Wilson for her warm and generous foreword; Brian Alderson for so generously sharing his apparently inexhaustive knowledge of children's publishing; Kate Wright for vital assistance with research and narrative development; David Foster, Kimberley Reynolds and Victor Watson for reading the text and making valuable suggestions and Laura Cecil for help with sourcing permissions and author portraits. Any remaining errors or omissions are my own.

Among my colleagues at Seven Stories I owe special thanks to Kate Edwards and Alison Gwynn, and to members of the Collection and Exhibitions team – Alison Fisher, Lindsey Gibson, Kris McKie, Gillian Rennie and Paula Wride; also to Carey Fluker-Hunt and David Wright who worked on the 'Picture book in Progress' project.

Thanks to Les Golding Photography, Tyne and Wear Archives and Museums and Damien Wootten for photography and scanning.

To Nicolette Winterbottom for sharing memories of her mother Ruth Gervis, and to Paul Gervis for scanning Ruth's self-portrait; and to Alan Garner for permission to quote from his correspondence with Michael Foreman.

Above all I am grateful to Deirdre McDermott, trustee of Seven Stories and picture book Publisher at Walker Books, for her energy, vision and determination to transform my initial ideas into something much more interesting. Sarah Pannasch deserves a special mention for her contribution to the design of this book. We've all had such fun working on this!

Thanks also to other members of the team at Walker Books, in particular Alan Lee, Tanya Rosie, Suzanne King, Maria Tunney, Sorrel Packham, Andy Soameson, Alice Primmer and Andrea Aboagye.

Finally, my family have been immensely tolerant and supportive of all of the extra work that this project has entailed. Thank you Robert, Thomas and Emma.

Copyright permissions

Seven Stories would like to thank all the rights holders who have generously granted permission for their work to be reproduced in this publication. Details of all the relevant rights holders are given below:

1	Artwork by **HELEN CRAIG** for *Angelina Ballerina* (1983) written by Katherine Holabird © Helen Craig.
3	Illustration by **EDWARD ARDIZZONE** for *The Little Train* (1946) written by Graham Greene © Estate of Edward Ardizzone 1973 and reproduced by permission of Penguin Random House UK.
5	Illustration by **RUTH GERVIS** for *Ballet Shoes* (1936) written by Noel Streatfeild © Orion Publishing Group and reproduced by kind permission.
8–9	Cover design by **HAROLD JONES** for *Lavender's Blue* (1954) compiled by Kathleen Lines © Estate of Harold Jones and reproduced by permission of Oxford University Press.
11–13	Illustrations by **RUTH GERVIS** for *Ballet Shoes* (1936) written by Noel Streatfeild © Orion Publishing Group reproduced by kind permission. Cover designs for the 1949 and 1957 Puffin editions reproduced by permission of Penguin Books Ltd.
14–17	Illustrations, manuscript and cover designs by **HAROLD JONES** for *The Visit to the Farm* (1939) and *The Enchanted Night* (1947) © Estate of Harold Jones.
18–21	Decorated letter from **HARMSEN VAN DER BEEK** to Enid Blyton, and illustration from *Here Comes Noddy Again* (1951) written by Enid Blyton © Classic Media. Illustrations by **EILEEN SOPER** for *The Toys Come to Life* (1943) written by Enid Blyton reproduced by permission of Chris Beetles and the Enid Blyton Estate.
22–25	Illustrations and cover design by **DOROTHY CRAIGIE** for *The Little Train* (1946) written by Graham Greene © Estate of Dorothy Craigie (presumed). Cover design (1973) by **EDWARD ARDIZZONE** © Estate of Edward Ardizzone, 1973 and reproduced by permission of Penguin Random House UK.
26–29	Illustrations by **EDWARD ARDIZZONE** for *Tim and Charlotte* (1951) and *Tim in Danger* (1953) © Estate of Edward Ardizzone, 1951 and 1953, and reproduced by permission of Frances Lincoln Children's Books. Preparatory artwork (dummy) for *Tim and Charlotte* © Estate of Edward Ardizzone.
30–31	Illustration and cover design by **JAN ORMEROD** for *Sunshine* (1981) © Estate of Jan Ormerod and reproduced by permission of Frances Lincoln Children's Books.
32–35	Preparatory artwork and final cover design by **SHIRLEY HUGHES** for *Lucy and Tom's Day* (1960) © Shirley Hughes.
36–39	Illustrations by **ANTONY MAITLAND** for *Mrs Cockle's Cat* (1961) written by Philippa Pearce © Antony Maitland.
40–43	Unpublished illustrations by **FAITH JAQUES** for *Charlie and the Chocolate Factory* (1967) written by Roald Dahl, and manuscript letter by Faith Jaques (c.1973) © Estate of Faith Jaques; published illustration and cover design for 1973 Puffin edition used with permission from Penguin Books Ltd.
44–49	Illustrations by **JUDITH KERR** for *The Tiger who Came to Tea* (1968) and *Mog the Forgetful Cat* (1970) © Kerr-Kneale Productions Limited. Childhood drawings (1930s) © Judith Kerr.
50–53	Illustrations by **MICHAEL FOREMAN** for *The Stone Book* (1976) and *Tom Fobble's Day* (1977 and Fontana Lions 1979 paperback edition), both written by Alan Garner © Michael Foreman. Cover designs for *The Stone Book* (1976), *Granny Reardun* (1977), *Tom Fobble's Day* (1977) and *The Aimer Gate* (1978) © Michael Foreman and reproduced with permission from HarperCollins Ltd.

54–57   Illustrations by **JOHN BURNINGHAM** for unpublished title *The Park* (c.1975), and published and unpublished illustrations for *The Dog* (1975) and *The Rabbit* (1974) © John Burningham.

58–61   Illustrations, preparatory artwork and cover design by **JOHN LAWRENCE** for *Rabbit and Pork* (1975) and illustrations for *The Christmas Cat* (1991) written by Robert Westall © John Lawrence.

62–65   Illustrations, preparatory artwork, layout and cover designs by **ROBERT CROWTHER** for *The Most Amazing Hide-and-Seek Alphabet Book* (1977) © Robert Crowther.

66–69   Illustrations and preparatory artwork by **JAN ORMEROD** for *Sunshine* (1981) © Estate of Jan Ormerod.

70–73   Illustrations and preparatory artwork by **PAT HUTCHINS** for *1 Hunter* (1985) © Pat Hutchins. Cover design reproduced with permission from Penguin Random House.

74–79   Illustrations, preparatory artwork and cover design by **HELEN CRAIG** for *Angelina Ballerina* (1983) written by Katharine Holabird © Helen Craig.

80–83   Illustrations by **GILLIAN MCCLURE** for *Tog the Ribber* (1985) written by Paul Coltman © Gillian McClure.

84–87   Illustrations and preparatory artwork by **ANGELA BARRETT** for *The Snow Queen* (1988) written by Naomi Lewis © Angela Barrett.

88–89   Illustration and cover design by **BOB GRAHAM** for *Jethro Byrde, Fairy Child* (2002) © Bob Graham and used by permission of Walker Books Ltd.

90–93   Illustrations and preparatory artwork by **SARAH GARLAND** for *Billy and Belle* (1992) © Sarah Garland. Cover design (2004) reproduced with permission from Frances Lincoln Children's Books.

94–99   Illustrations and preparatory artwork by **KIM LEWIS** for *Floss* (1993) © Kim Lewis. Cover illustration © 1993 Kim Lewis and reproduced by permission of Walker Books Ltd.

100–103 Illustrations and preparatory artwork by **BOB GRAHAM** for *Jethro Byrde, Fairy Child* (2002) © Bob Graham and used by permission of Walker Books Ltd.

104–107 Illustrations by **NICK SHARRATT** for *Starring Tracy Beaker* (2006) written by Jacqueline Wilson © Nick Sharratt. Cover design reproduced with permission from Penguin Random House UK.

108–111 Illustrations and preparatory artwork by **MICK MANNING** and **BRITA GRANSTRÖM** for *Greek Hero* (2007) © Mick Manning and Brita Granström. Cover design reproduced with permission from Frances Lincoln Children's Books.

112–115 Illustrations and preparatory artwork by **POLLY DUNBAR** for *My Dad's a Birdman* (2007) written by David Almond © Polly Dunbar. Cover illustration © 2007 Polly Dunbar and reproduced by permission of Walker Books Ltd.

116–119 Preparatory artwork by **YASMEEN ISMAIL** for *Time for Bed, Fred!* (2013) © Yasmeen Ismail. Cover design reproduced by permission of Bloomsbury Children's Books.

128   Illustration by **EDWARD ARDIZZONE** for *Tim in Danger* (1953) © Estate of Edward Ardizzone and reproduced by permission of Frances Lincoln Children's Books.

Every effort has been made to contact all the relevant copyright holders, but should there be any errors or omissions Seven Stories would be pleased to insert the appropriate acknowledgement in any subsequent edition of the book.

'Tired as she was, Charlotte had to peel lots of potatoes.'
Final artwork by Edward Ardizzone for *Tim in Danger* (1953)